Practicing Silence

Practicing Silence
Poems

Jon G. Jackson

Ink Monkey Press

Published in USA by Ink Monkey Press
©2022 Jon G. Jackson

All rights reserved. No part of this book may be
reproduced or transmitted, in any form or by any means,
without permission of the author.

Ink Monkey Press
P.O. Box 11435
Santa Rosa, CA 95406
www.ArtandPoetry.com
jacksojg@gmail.com

First Edition
1 3 5 7 9 10 8 6 4 2

Paperback: ISBN 978-0-9840172-4-9
Hardback: ISBN 978-0-9840172-5-6

There is a simultaneous inscribed and numbered limited edition
hardback of twenty-five copies.

Cover image: "Reflections" ©2022 Jon G. Jackson
Book design: Sherrie Lovler
Font: Brioso Pro designed by Robert Slimbach for Adobe Systems

For Sherrie
My Co-Conspirator & True Partner

TABLE OF CONTENTS

Introduction 1

I Heard Frogs Tonight 5
Fish Faces 7
Look At The Stars 9
Why I Cry 11
The Fifth Glass 13
What I Wanted 15
The Need That Can Only Be Met 17
A Sonnet For Eurydice 19
Sirens 21
The Trumpets Of Bezalel 23
God In The Room Next Door 25
Eve 27
Who Told You You Were Naked? 29
The Tale Of Noah 31
Prodigal Son 35
There Comes A Time 37
Showtime 39
Nothing Is Far In Mayreau 43
Bird Buddha 45
On My Island 47
Stars On A Rainy Night 49
Practicing Silence 51

Acknowledgments 53
Publishing Credits 55

INTRODUCTION

When I was younger, I always wanted to write prose. I saw myself writing science fiction and strange psychological tales. Stories abounded in my imagination, and they still do. Writing prose didn't really happen, though I've never lost that long-held passion. But, meanwhile, in the last fifteen years, I more or less fell into writing poetry. And what a gift this has been! I'm tempted to say this was never what I imagined. Yet, in fact, it's exactly what I wanted. I just didn't know it.

So, the question is and always is: what to write? There are problems in the world, and difficulties that people face in their everyday lives. And there is profound beauty, and love. And there are many ways of making a difference. Where to begin? Each of us, I believe, must follow our own personal path in life. There is no other. Going any other way, while not the worst mistake you'll make, will not result in soul-making. Each of us must speak the thing we simply cannot keep silent. So, just say it.

And that's what I do here in the pages you're about to read. Life is broad and deep, and it speaks with many voices, as it goes by many names. Silence will teach us, most of all, what we need to know. Wherever you might find that in these poems, dive in there. Go as far as you can and breathe in underwater. Swim. Explore. Take your time. There's no need to rush to the surface. The poems will still be here.

Practicing Silence

I HEARD FROGS TONIGHT

I heard frogs tonight
in the field to the south.
And again, two hours later,
slightly to the right.
A long jump, the full moon obscured.

Practicing Silence

FISH FACES

Look at the fish faces clamoring.
Lips above water, wanting to kiss.
Dozens with wings, and more all the time—
Like koi in a pond, where I'm from.

Fins fluttering, reflections ripple.
One hundred wide eyes
stare wildly at the bright green sky.
A gust of fingers blows through my hair.

Held close by the mountain,
this valley, they say,
is empty now. No more visitors.
Nothing to do here.

Kiss, kiss, kiss, kiss.
I can't walk away.
They follow with every step,
and fly to my dreams.

Practicing Silence

LOOK AT THE STARS

Look at the stars.
Don't name them.
Go way past what you know.
Look at the stars.
What do you see?

What visions appear?
Are they dancing?
What riddles duly speak?
Show me the crawling beasts.
What do you see?

Do you hear voices
calling your name?
Do they reach for your heart,
parading truth?
What do you see?

Just look. Take just
one step further.
Put your knowledge aside
and push open the next veil.
What do you see?

The deepest You abounds.
The Id can't help but sing.
The Shadow plays.
It's all and all a living thing.
What do you see?

Do you see stars?
Well, they see you.
Do you see dreams?
Just look at the stars.
What do you see?

Practicing Silence

WHY I CRY

I don't cry over losses.
I cry when reminded of love.
That it exists. That it's mine, in my heart.

I don't cry over things I've never had.
I cry for what I have right now.
In my hand. Here, in front of me.

My tears resist death and dying.
They just won't show themselves.
For injustice. Or personal wrong.

But they flow uncontrollably
At a soft loving touch.
Whispered sounds.
I'm here. No need to worry.

I don't cry at goodbyes.
But I weep for hellos.
Even when no word is spoken.

Practicing Silence

THE FIFTH GLASS

This afternoon, my ex-wife came to visit
with her new wife. And we all
set up a table on the back porch.

We were having wine and cheese
purchased on our long trip,
a big loop locally. And we all, somehow,
thought we were one wine glass short.

When we talked about it later,
we all agreed: Yes, they had told me
to bring the glass out, and, yes, I did.
Like we were one glass short.

And, yet, there were only four of us.
In attentive silence, we examined
that fifth glass — the one that
all of us said was missing.

Then we clinked our glasses, and we
shared that wine amongst ourselves —
a good one, from a Calistoga winery.

And we all said,
"Well, she's not here, anyway…"

Practicing Silence

WHAT I WANTED

Why is it that people always say:
I wanted to ask you — or
I wanted to say — or
I wanted it to suggest something else?

I always wonder: When did you
want that? Yesterday? Last week?
Last year? Or, maybe you mean it's a
constant craving over a long piece of time?

When I turn back to my monkey business,
people seem puzzled, mouth half-open.
But, they will say: *I wanted...*
I reply: *Yes, oh yes. I heard you.*

The past wants desperately to hold us,
as if with blindfolds and gags,
and lethal loyalty to old, old tales
which actually died long, long ago.

Isn't it time now to stand up,
and step forward in the here and now?
To be present in your experience.
And finally say, if even a whisper: *I want?*

Practicing Silence

THE NEED THAT CAN ONLY BE MET

You've probably heard, as have I,
that humans are essentially religious.
That deep in our souls, if not in our minds,
we find communion with things divine.

You've probably felt, as have I,
an essential longing, an open heart,
A want and need which, they say,
can only be met by perfect divine love.

And you've probably been told, as have I,
this somehow proves that God exists.
That we are his or her created children,
and that the universe itself loves us.

I've no problem that our souls are religious,
most especially when I play my guitar.
I am perfectly convinced this yearning exists,
and it needs, in fact, a perfect divine love.

But, my friends, this is the human condition.
Our predicament. We have this perfect need
that can only be met by such a love.
When, in fact, no such love exists at all.

And this is why, and I mean this,
there is no opting out. It comes down to us!
It's up to us to live love and caring,
to refuse hate, to stand against cruelty.

It's all human nature, after all.
The Holocaust was not an aberration.
But neither is love and beauty.
Where do you stand, my friend?

We must create the We.
We must stay open to our pain.
We must build our bold community.
Not perfect. Not divine. But together.

Because it's true, so very much the case.
You can have faith in this.
It can and will only come from us.
And we have a need that can only be met.

Practicing Silence

A SONNET FOR EURYDICE

Recall the time we swam beneath the wave.
We never thought of air is something we
might need, and never lived in time. The sea
was all we breathed, and all that Nature ever gave.

And then we went our sep'rate ways. Oh, woe!
Yes, you to Hades' secret lair, and I,
while playing lyric songs, consumed, did die
a thousand deaths, each one another low.

But, when I came, at last, my life so gone,
and you fell back along our trek, you sang
out Hermes' name! Oh, he it was who turned

to look! And as he fell, we then moved on
together to the light. Then strings did hang
above the fire…oh, where they nicely burned!

Practicing Silence

SIRENS

What exactly did the Sirens sing?
"Hello, boys! Come on back!"
We are told it meant
crashing the ship offshore.

But, is this true?
What would the Sirens say?
"They made so many promises!
So tied to the mast!"

Were they expressing
their hearts' desires?
Unimaginable sound?
A chorus of ocean?

Probably...
But the ship sailed on past.

So, everyone loved the sun.
So warm. So dry.
Almost time now
to go home underwater.

Practicing Silence

THE TRUMPETS OF BEZALEL
(After Rilke)

"The Trumpets of Bezalel" by Tim Holmes

You know her voice, her face,
her raspberry lips in bloom.
The hearth burns in her heart,
and in her womb.

The trumpets flair as she dances.
Bosom bare, she winds and twirls,
her desire so clear.
The ceremony has begun.

Movement in such metal,
her arms curved like a cove.
Nothing can hide her feline grace.

Without restraint, a formless void.
The moon winks her approval.
Your life will never be the same.

Practicing Silence

GOD IN THE ROOM NEXT DOOR

The deep thunder of your shuffling feet
has kept me awake now for hours!
You and your party angels,
eating apples from Eden,
and drunk on gallons of ambrosia.

The constant singing is driving me mad!
You and your heavenly chorus, and those
long songs all about what a great guy you are!
Songs that crash through every boundary made
    in a lifetime,
and every wall so carefully built, brick by brick.

Every wall, that is, except the one that separates
    us now.
You in your room, and I in mine.
The wall I pound on to get you to stop!
Shut the fuck up! And turn the volume down!
I'm trying to sleep, damn it!

I can see now why you don't return my calls.
Never send a text. Or reply to my long lonely letters.
I laugh with bitter tears at tales that God is dead.
Dead drunk is what I would say!
You and your friends...who don't include me...

My fists beat against the rhythm, my voice
    hoarse.
Are you deaf? That alone must certainly
    draw your attention!
That muffled arrhythmia. My constant cries.

But, no...
The angels come and go,
the chorus like an ocean's surge.
The walls fall, one by one.
Except for this one.
The one that separates us now.

Practicing Silence

EVE

In our mythology, our literature, our world,
there is at least one woman
who never experienced the loss of her mother.
And that would be Eve.

I say "at least" because
the same would be true of Lilith.
But, that's another story, more hidden,
and not "official," as it were.

Not just the loss—
the experience of a mother.
Our unconscious memories of womb—
our infant's recollection of face.

To say nothing of how she fed us,
raised us, taught us, created us.
As we flailed through adolescence,
repeating her own personal mistakes.

Our rebellion and disavowal.
Our rejections of her, her life experience.
How it all came together, one way or another,
and we finally saw her, the woman that she is.

Perhaps too late? Or, maybe not?
But, Eve never knew her mother.
Never had a mother. Any mother.
She was the only one, the only woman.

Imagine having to figure that out
on your own. No one before you
to tell you it was normal, alas.
And tell you to be proud of who you are.

Practicing Silence

WHO TOLD YOU YOU WERE NAKED?

Of all the words, all the things,
of all the sounds one could have made—
Why this? Why this commentary on nakedness?

That place of no control,
of open truth,
where someone could, yes,
really hurt you.

Who told you you were naked?
Who said the blows and the arrows
would defeat you?
Could defeat you?
Who said that?

There was fruit today
in our morning meal.
And as knowledge arose,
seeing difference for the first time,
we somehow thought of figs.

Practicing Silence

THE TALE OF NOAH

Imagine Noah at the end of the Ice Age.
The glaciers are melting, seas rising.
Atlantis has gone under water.
Civilizations are drowning, or learning to swim.
Everything is changing, new maps drawn.
His sons report warmer weather
all over the known world.

An ocean of water sits high above the valley,
it's icy lip thinning as danger looms.
He wants to save his animals from the flood.
So, he builds a boat that will only float.
His daughters report dying crops.
Men all around call him mad.

One day, the ice rim cracks, the frigid water
sitting poised, ready to fill the void.
It is time. He leads his animals
into the massive zoo, meticulously tailored.
His men report eminent disaster.
The ice rim cracks again.

At the foot of the valley is a stone wall,
miles long.
Solid, firm, two hundred yards high.
It was made by men to keep strangers out.
But today it will also keep the water in.
His animals report anxious dis-ease.
And the flooding begins.

The first torrent slams the heavy door shut.
The huge vessel spins like a top.
Men are thrown overboard into violent waves.
The border wall holds, the village is destroyed.
They all hear reports of snapping trees
as the vessel lifts and floats.

For days they drift ever closer to the wall.
The new lake breaches, creating waterfalls.
Outside, all see the bobbing ship high above,
expecting it to fall, come crashing down.
Soldiers report evacuations.
All hangs tense and beautiful.

Practicing Silence

Finally, a tunnel through the wall gives way.
The drain begins, a new river rushes out.
What was old washes away, destroyed.
But the huge wall stands firm, strong.
The shamans report sunny skies
as everything changes.

Weeks later, the water is only slightly down.
The boat is grounded on the valley's arm.
All is intact, no one else has died.
Noah finally opens the door as silence abounds.
His wife reports that she is pregnant.
And the sky is a new strange blue.

Practicing Silence

THE PRODIGAL SON

I was the prodigal son.
And when I came home,
honestly, to give of myself,
and to care for another,
that other was my mother,
and I saw no fatted calf.

She begged me
to bring her drugs,
to overdose,
since I was a physician.

And I said, "No."
And, instead, listened
to her left big toe—
ingrown, inflamed,
her constant strain.

And I dug into that,
literally, as a physician,
with nothing but my hands,
and a simple instrument.

She yelled at me,
this woman who never knew me,
this mother of mine,
with no fatted calf.

And I relieved her pain.

Practicing Silence

THERE COMES A TIME

There comes a time when you have to go back.
When you have to be who you were.
Who you are now.
It's not a question of choice.

All this time spent being someone else,
well, it was training. It was practice.
Because it took a lot of skill to do that,
and you really could use that now.

So many times, trying to fit,
wanting approval. Just wanting to be.
You didn't know that it's right here.
Not around the corner.

It was right here at your fingers,
all that time. You think I'm wrong?
Well, then, go your way.
Live that life. The other life.

But there does come a time, yes, it does,
when nothing else will do.
So, just remember. Remember.
Just what you want. And who you are.

Practicing Silence

SHOWTIME

Are we ready to step aside
and let the other speak?
Through our children?
Through the ones
they've said don't matter?
Through the ones that say,
Me, Too to the vacant void?

Through the ones that die every day,
everywhere, around the world,
to whom we say, *We support you!*
as they fall? And they say,
No, you never will, and
No, you never have.

Are we ready to let
another species awaken us
to things we've always
said we believe?
The ones who say, *You hypocrites!*
You who settled for
soft beds, and something
supposedly normal.

Are we ready to say, *Enough!*
as others have always said,
time and again, with no credibility?
Those whom we say we must help,
but never do, not really?

Can we give up our comfortable lives,
our dominion? We thought what we did
so long ago made us worthy.
But, are we willing now to lay it down?
Our reputations, our careers,
our safety? All on the line?

Are we willing to take a stand,
again, at last, after so many years?
We thought we won back then.
We'd done our part,
and there was nothing more.
So, are we?

Practicing Silence

If not, you know,
our children will die,
our spouses demeaned.
Our dark selves will lay in the streets,
dead, as thousands spit and sink
into poverty and shit.

And you. You will go on
in your comfortable life
until, one day, you
are brought down, too.

Believe me. Please.
Our large work was never finished.
It has, again, been
thrown to the ground.
And it will happen again,
unless you wake up now.
Unless you say, *Enough!* Now!
At what is in front of you.

Practicing Silence

NOTHING IS FAR
IN MAYREAU

The womb is unnamed as you begin.
Steep hills are the forward path, but
there is an easier one behind you.
Though you'll never see the keys there.

The oppressive heat is like the palm
of a hand standing between you
and the goals you have chosen. No wind
to lift you. Only scattered shade.

You look up and think of what they say,
"Nothing is far in Mayreau."
But, why not turn and stay near the water?
You don't really need to see the keys.

Or do you? So, you climb, step-by-step,
and each peak you reach leads only
to a turn in the road, and the next
to another. But still you climb.

At the top, you pause to consider.
And you look back down the way you came.
You trusted too long in raw fortune.
Your goal requires an active will.

Back down the hill is a church.
The grounds there offer a better shade.
Bird-like music flows through the trees.
A stony path winds past the door.

So, it can't be far now, can it?
Through the trees, under a blue sky,
the palm now protects you from behind.
Here is the garden, and the keys.

From start to peak, to the garden path,
with one mistake along the way.
It's true, nothing is far in Mayreau.
You simply have to find a way.

Practicing Silence

BIRD BUDDHA

Why does he always go alone
on his birding quests,
deep into the pulsing wood
to hear a symphony of sound?

'Cause that's when his feathers
come out, and he glides up
to the verdant trees
and watches humans instead.

He feels his dino blood.
He hears the sunlight.
Lured by magnetic poles
calling him, and calling.

He fluffs himself up
and stretches his wings
and flies to South America.
Hopefully home in time for dinner.

Practicing Silence

ON MY ISLAND

If you take your shoes off,
you're not just on ground anymore.
You enter in where everything's alive.

How sweet to be surrounded by water,
as it calls your name and sighs at your feet.
The horizon beckons, and the water behind you,
on the other side of the breathing mountain,
says, "No worries, bro! I've got you covered."

You won't know what's East or West,
'cause there's only the ocean and the folded hills.
Birds will say, "Relax. Let go."

And the wind will lift you up with wings
to the other shore, and set you down on living soil.
And you'll hear the waves where you just came from
say, "Easy, bro. I've got your back."

Practicing Silence

STARS ON A RAINY NIGHT

Where do they go,
Those starry stars,
Those winking lights,
Those distant suns,
Lanterns of the night?

They fall to earth,
As drops of life,
And flow as streams,
To open seas,
Back to the sky.

Practicing Silence

PRACTICING SILENCE

The dead cat sits
by the side of the road
practicing silence.

Practicing Silence

ACKNOWLEDGEMENTS

Deep-hearted thanks to Sherrie Lovler for all her time and support, and for her belief in me. And more thanks for her editing and design skills, and for publishing this book through Ink Monkey Press.

Sincere thanks to Les Bernstein and Fran Claggett-Holland for first publishing several of these poems through The Redwood Writers, and for their editing and consistently wise advice.

Special thanks also to Larry Robinson, who sent out many of my poems to his online readers, and for his poetry salons in Sebastopol, California.

I have great gratitude for the opportunities to share my poems with two poetry groups, one in Santa Rosa, California, and the other through the O'Hanlon Center for the Arts in Mill Valley, California.

Practicing Silence

PUBLISHING CREDITS

"I Heard Frogs Tonight" was first published in a *Poem In Your Pocket* chapbook, Berkeley Public Library, 2019.

"Prodigal Son," "A Sonnet For Eurydice," and "Why I Cry" were first published in *Crow: In the Light of Day, In the Dark of Night*, Redwood Writers 2019 Poetry Anthology, Redwood Writers Press, Santa Rosa, California.

"The Tale Of Noah," "The Fifth Glass," "Nothing Is Far In Mayreau," "Eve," and "Showtime" were first published in *And Yet*, Redwood Writers 2020 Poetry Anthology, Redwood Writers Press, Santa Rosa, California.

"What I Wanted" was first published in *Beyond Distance*, Redwood Writers 2021 Poetry Anthology, Redwood Writers Press, Santa Rosa, California.

"The Tale Of Noah" was additionally published in the Sonoma County poetry anthology, *The Freedom of New Beginnings*, edited by Phyllis Meshulam, Poetry Crossing Press, 2022.

"Stars On A Rainy Night" was first published in *Crossroads*, Redwood Writers 2022 Poetry Anthology, Redwood Writers Press, Santa Rosa, California.

Jon G. Jackson is a retired psychiatrist and depth psychotherapist, and an award-winning poet. He is a former Chair of the Numina Center for Spirituality & the Arts. He currently facilitates a Rainer Maria Rilke reading group sponsored by the Friends of the San Francisco Jung Institute. He has taught two ten-lecture courses: "Rilke's Letters to a Young Poet" and "A Psychological Approach to the Old Testament." He currently teaches a shorter course on Rilke for the Osher Lifelong Learning Institute at Sonoma State University and at Dominican University.

www.ingramcontent.com/pod-product-compliance
Lightning Source LLC
Chambersburg PA
CBHW032051290426
44110CB00012B/1041